Filey

A Practical Guide
for Visitors

**compiled and illustrated by
Ted Gower**

DALESMAN BOOKS
1983

The Dalesman Publishing Company Ltd.,
Clapham, via Lancaster, LA2 8EB.

First published 1977
Second edition 1983

ISBN: 0 85206 737 2

Printed in Great Britain by
GEORGE TODD & SON
Marlborough Street, Whitehaven

CONTENTS

Introduction 4

General Information 4

Today and Yesterday 6

Filey in History 8

"Nobbut Just" 11

The Coble Landing 12

The Brigg 13

Fishermen and Fishing Boats 15

The Cobles 19

Wrecks 21

The Lifeboat 22

Filey's Parish Church 24

Places of Interest around Filey 26

Motor Runs 29

Walks 31

INTRODUCTION

A N ancient place, for centuries an important fishing town, Filey is loved for its beautiful and usually peaceful bay. From the rocky Brigg to the chalk cliffs of Flamborough, the sweeping sands gleam yellow in the sunshine, and the sea is often as blue as the Mediterranean. The town, smaller and quieter than its neighbours, Scarborough and Bridlington, has historic and charming corners. There are colourful gardens, and enough shops to satisfy the visitor who does not seek supermarkets.

The Romans and the Vikings knew it. Charlotte Brontë was fond of the place. Royalty have holidayed here. Many people look on it as a second home. This book aims to help the newcomer to enjoy a stay in Filey, and to join the ranks of enthusiasts.

I gratefully acknowledge help from Mr. Alan Dearden, Assistant County Librarian, Scarborough, and Mr. J. M. Fearon, Secretary of Filey Local History Society.

GENERAL INFORMATION

U NTIL 1974, Filey was an urban district in the East Riding of Yorkshire. With the abolition of the ancient Ridings, the town is now in North Yorkshire (the largest county, by area, in England) and linked with Scarborough and Whitby.

Postal Address: Filey, North Yorkshire.

Population: about 5,120. In 1812 it was 700.

Early closing: Wednesday.

Post Office: Murray Street (closes early on Saturdays).

Police: Murray Street.

Coast Guard: The Beach.

Railway Station: Station Avenue. Trains to Scarborough, Bridlington, Hull.

Buses: Station Avenue. Also Coach Station.

Car Parks: Station Avenue, Church Ravine, Coble Landing, Country Park on North Cliff (also caravans).

Cinema: The Grand, Union Street.

Theatre: The Brig, Station Avenue.

Crescent Gardens Sun Lounge (June to Sept.): Family revue, music hall, cabaret, etc.

Churches: St. Oswald's Parish Church. St. John's Church. Methodist, Roman Catholic, Salvation Army.

Folk Museum: Queen Street. Open daily except Saturday, end of May to mid-September.

Miniature Golf: Country Park; Glen Gardens.

Crazy Golf: Foreshore.

Putting: Country Park; Foreshore; Glen Gardens.

Tennis: Southdene (grass and hard courts).

Open-air draughts and table tennis: Glen Gardens.

Croquet Putt: Glen Gardens.

Pedal Boats and Children's Canoes: Glen Gardens.

Angling: From Brigg or by boat. Filey Fishing Festival early September.

Touring caravan and picnic sites: Country Park, North Cliff. Blue Dolphin, Gristhorpe. Crow's Nest, Gristhorpe. Reighton Sands. Cayton Bay.

Distances: Scarborough 7 miles. Bridlington 12 miles. York 40 miles.

INFORMATION CENTRE: John Street. Tel. 512204/72261.

TODAY AND YESTERDAY

MANY years ago I stayed in a little house in Queen Street, Filey, where I found a big welcome and marvellous meals. I've never forgotten the Yorkshire puddings. Served as a separate course, with gravy, they were a meal in themselves. In later years I stayed in similar houses in and around Queen Street, and had similar meals. No wonder, for the families were all related, and all vied with each other in maintaining a high standard. At another house, only a stone's throw away, I was asked what I would like for supper. After three big meals, I felt unable to eat anything. As I went upstairs, I heard the lady asking my wife if I was ill, as I had refused supper, or could she perhaps slip out for some fish and chips.?

I was once there on Lifeboat Day, when the maroons cracked over the town and the massive lifeboat on huge wood wheels was dragged round the town by clattering horses. The crowds on the pavement threw coins into the boat, and it was sunny and everyone was happy. But little Mrs. Jenkinson, whose husband was the lifeboat cox, said, "Aye, it's all very nice now, but when the maroon goes at two o'clock on a January morning, with a gale from the east, there's a different feeling. I've stood down there by the lamp, watching for t' boat coming back, and worrying if the crew were all safely in it." It was a reminder of how much the lives of the people in the old part of Filey were bound up with the sea.

The regular flashes over the bay at night, from Flamborough's lighthouse, or the moaning of the siren on the buoy at the end of the Brigg, indicate danger. The blue bay can be a fearsome destroyer at times, and the rocks of the Brigg have taken many ships and the lives of the crews.

On a sunny morning it is difficult to imagine danger. The sun streams across the water and the cobles are bright with light. I woke early one morning, and was slipping out for a walk before breakfast, when I met Mr. Jenkinson in the doorway. "It's been a grand day," he said. It was 7-30, but he had been out fishing since 4-30.

I walked on the sands for half an hour. They must be the finest in the country. For more than five miles they stretch away towards the tall cliffs at Bempton, clean and firm. Sometimes you have to search for a pebble. Even at Bank Holiday, when the crowds are there, you can soon leave them behind. As well as ponies and donkeys, kept by Mr. Burr, in those days there were little chariots, seating two children and pulled by small, well rounded ponies with long tails. There was a Punch and Judy show and the Pierrots. If rain stopped the performance it was transferred to the Grand Cinema, and I remember people sitting on the steps because all the seats were full. There were crowds on the beach in 1911 when Robert Blackburn, the aeroplane pioneer from Leeds, tried out his first monoplane.

There was a slipway at Primrose Valley, where the Romans probably had a pier. The Princess Royal used to send her sons to Filey, and they played on the beach, guarded by a governess. The same sands were busy in 1311, when a chest of gold florentines and silver coins was found, and claimed by the local landowner, Robert de Lacy, from Hunmanby. The crown, which was always arguing with the Lord of the Manor about wrecks, made an enquiry into the salvaged chest.

Wrecks were often looted. In 1344 a ship bound for London was driven ashore and boarded by 30 locals led by the gentry. The cargo was taken off. So was that of the barque "Martin" in 1542, when Filey folk took off fish, cloth, and £600 of Scottish merchants' money. I do not know if ships were deliberately lured on to the Brigg by false lights as was done on other parts of the Yorkshire Coast—perhaps there were enough wrecks without that.

Race horses from Malton are brought to Filey sands to exercise in winter, when their normal training ground is frozen.

FILEY IN HISTORY

THE name Filey has been interpreted by different authorities as meaning a "slim finger of land", from file; or "fowl pasture", from Fucelac in Domesday Book. William le Gros, Lord of Holderness and Earl of Albemarle and York, who commenced the building of Scarborough castle, acquired a house in Filey in 1140. Henry II took the lands from Albemarle and developed the town of Scarborough.

The area was populated, however, long before the Normans. There was a Roman signal station on Carr Naze, above the Brigg. Carr is from an ancient British word "caer", meaning camp. Further back still, the discovery at nearby Gristhorpe of the skeleton of a man wrapped in skins, with a bronze weapon by his side, indicates habitation 3,000 years ago. The Bay has changed since Ice Age days. The river Derwent, which now flows westward through the Vale of Pickering to Malton, once emptied in Filey Bay. Blocked by glacial drift, it formed Pickering Lake between the hills west of Scarborough and the Wolds behind Bridlington.

The Vikings raided the area and then settled. Flamborough was called "Little Denmark" at one time, and it has been said the fishermen of Filey and Flamborough show Viking descent. Their boats, the "cobles", certainly, have developed from the Viking long ship. The local dialect contains Scandinavian words.

Filey had a market charter in 1221, but the burgesses of Scarborough, fearing competition, had it revoked. The discovery of a chalybeate spring containing iron salts started the spa attraction. As early as 1700 people came to cure apoplexy, epilepsy, asthma, and "hypochondriac melancholy and windiness". Scarborough developed its spa on a big scale, and the council tried to prevent abuses in the sale of bottled spa water. Filey's spa was on Carr Naze, but no traces remain. There was a scheme to pipe the water to a more convenient situation near the sands, and Mr. Munro, a surgeon, lent out a portable bath and offered bathing accommodation in his house.

New houses were built about that time, and one in Church Street bears the date 1705. Only the wealthy could have travelled any distance to take the waters. There were no railways and, apart from walking, horse or horse-drawn coaches were the only means of transport. Royal Union stage coaches from Scarborough to Hull arrived in Filey at 8 a.m. on Mondays, Wednesdays and Fridays. The "Original British Queen" from Scarborough passed through Filey at 11 a.m. on Tuesdays, Thursdays and Saturdays, returning at 4-30 p.m. There were four inns—Foords, Ship, Britannai and Packhorse. The railway came in 1846-7 and visitors began to arrive in crowds. The station, although it had only two platforms, had a vaulted roof. The line, to Scarborough and Bridlington, is still open, despite many threats of closure.

The large buildings on the cliff top began to rise, in late Georgian style. The new road was called the Crescent, although it is hardly that shape. Some of the houses have iron balconies and imposing stucco fronts. Then came early Victorian houses, with basements; many of them are now

FOLK MUSEUM

converted into holiday flats. Cliff House in Belle Vue Street (originally North Street), which was a favourite place of Charlotte Brontë, is now a cafe. At Black Cliff Head is a large neo-Tudor house, built in 1891, with splendid gardens down to the Beach. It is now a convalescent home for one of the printing trade unions. A town bellman, Robert Stalk, rang his brass bell in the Crescent Gardens and announced items lost by visitors. Coal for the town came by ship, and carts unloaded it on the beach.

Foords Hotel in Queen Street is late Georgian and has Grecian Doric columns at the door. At the seaward end of Queen Street is an ancient house, once "T'awd Ship Inn", which is reputed to have been the haunt of smugglers and to have had secret cupboards. Some of the terraced houses in the same street have coloured panels in the doors depicting fishing boats. The backyards are full of fishing gear. Part of this area, for long the home of the fishing community, has been demolished, and new houses and flats, doubtless more convenient if less picturesque, have been built. Intermarriage has been common, and family names such as Jenkinson, Cammish and Cappleman are numerous. They take pride in being "Fyla bred and born".

At the inland end of Queen Street is the museum, opened in 1970 and formed from two old cottages dating from 1696. One of them was a dairy, with cows in the backyard. A panel on the front wall reads: "The fear of God be in you." Although small, the museum is packed with items of local interest—domestic, fishing and farming. There are many fascinating photographs. Filey Local History Society is responsible for the museum, which is open daily except Saturday. The market cross stood near here, but disappeared in Victorian development.

CHURCH HILL.

"NOBBUT JUST"

AT the seaward end of Queen Street is a lamp with a red panel. This can be seen out at sea, and acts as a guide for incoming boats. Nearby, round the corner, are some seats with a fine sea view; they are much favoured by elderly fishermen, who sit in the morning sun with caps tilted over their eyes gazing out over the Bay. Steps lead down from here to the Coble Landing.

Church Street leads off the top of Queen Street, down the hill to the Ravine which is crossed by a bridge. There are several charming old cottages here. The bridge, which replaced one destroyed by a storm in 1857, is the way to the church. It used to be said of someone near death that he would soon be "going over into t' North Riding". The county boundary was marked by the Ravine, and the churchyard was over the boundary. A Filey fisherman was once asked if he lived in the East Riding. "Nobbut just", he replied. An engraving of about 1828 shows the Ravine completely without trees. Number 45, Church Street, or Church Hill, bears a plate on the wall stating that this 17th century cottage was restored in 1946 by J. Needham. It is scheduled as a building of historic interest.

At one time this cottage was a farmstead. Cows grazed in the field behind, where bungalows now stand. In August there was a fair, and Corrigans, the fair people, connected their hose pipes to the cottage tap. The Corrigan family are still in the amusement business on the Yorkshire coast. In the yard at the back of the cottage was the toilet, called by Fila folk "t' backway". The cobble stones in front were kept clear of grass by prodding with kitchen forks. The Pashby family, who lived there, made a special effort to remove every blade of grass for the third Sunday in June, which was the Sunday School Anniversary. "Liz Ann", old Grandma Pashby, was an expert knitter of fishermen's jerseys, although she had only one hand. Filey had its own jersey patterns—one was a zig-zag design, said to be suggested by the twisting cliff paths.

THE COBLE LANDING

THE name has nothing to do with the large stones forming the slope on which the boats are kept. It refers to the boats, which are "cobles". This unique open sea boat is peculiar to the North East coast, and especially to Yorkshire. The landing was once referred to as "Pampletine". The story is that around 1850 a fisherman saw the landing littered with lines, warps, nets and other gear, and said, "Ah've nivver seen such a pampletine mess iv all mi life". The name is still given to the cliffs behind the landing.

The lifeboat house is here, and the tractors which launch both it and the cobles are kept nearby. At one time there was little else but huts for fishing gear, but there is now a cafe and beach chalets. I have seen the landing crowded with boats, and many more pulled up the Ravine which was once a sandy road. A new sea wall was built in 1896 and the present lifeboat house erected.

The promenade has areas of grass and is mostly free from traffic. At the southern end, where Crescent Hill ascends steeply to the town, is Royal Parade, at the foot of tree-shaded Martin's Ravine. There used to be a wooden structure here, which gave the feeling of being on a ship. Plans were made just after the last war to extend the promenade round the Bay to Hunmanby Gap, but these have not materialised. The Crescent Gardens are bright with flowers, and the view over the Bay to the white cliffs of Flamborough is splendid. In the gardens is the Sun Lounge, with a cafe. Concerts are held here.

There are steep footpaths and steps down to the Beach (the name given to the promenade road). They climb through the trees giving glimpses of the Bay. Cargate Hill, once known as Kye Gate, leading down to the Beach from Murray Street, is steep, and the unique raised footpaths are steeper. The first lifeboat house was at the bottom. At the top of this hill at the corner of John Street is the Information Centre, with grassy slopes and gardens on the seaward side. At one time it was a convent school, and the nuns, with their tall head dresses, were often seen in the town.

THE BRIGG

IN 1828 it was called the Bridge, but its origins are probably from the Scandinavian "Bryggja", meaning jetty or landing place. Bridge is from Old English "Brycg". Legend has it that the devil started to build the Brigg to cross the North Sea but tired and dropped his hammer. Trying to find it, he instead picked a haddock. The fish still bears his fingerprints today. The massive steps of Lower Calcareous gritstone stretch out from the boulder clay cliffs, and are a hazard for shipping as well as shelter for the Bay. When the sea is rough, spray is flung to spectacular heights as the waves hit the angled rocks. The pools are many and well populated. Round the corner they increase in size, and have names such as the Emperor's Bath in

FILEY BRIGG

which Constantine is said to have bathed. The Brigg is fascinating to explore, but be careful of the tides. People have been swept to their deaths by big waves, even at low water. Many have been trapped, and rescued with difficulty by coastguards. The cliffs are of oolitic limestone, created by tiny sea creatures, invisible to the naked eye but fascinating through a microscope.

Running south is a pier of stone called the Spittal. It could be natural, or it may have been built by the Romans to form a harbour. The Romans certainly had a signal tower on Carr Naze. Erosion took away the building, but socket stones have been discovered in which pillars supporting the first floor stood. Pottery and coins have also been unearthed.

There was a scheme to develop the Brigg into a huge harbour that would shelter a fleet of ships. The company was formed in 1876, with £100,000 capital. Its announcement caused jubilation in Filey and the streets were decked with flags. It came to naught, however, and the Brigg remains a wonderful place for holiday-makers, anglers and botanists. Seabirds haunt it, and seals can sometimes be seen.

I once went back to Filey from the Brigg in a coble called "Faith". Halfway across the Bay the engine stopped, and an old lady expressed concern. The fisherman laughed at her, and joked about the coble's name. He then primed the engine, which eventually started, and we went on our way. At one time a rowing boat carried tired visitors back from the Brigg. The stalwart oarsman, pulling a heavy boat with a dozen or more passengers, had forearms like tree trunks. On beaching, he carried people on his back through the shallow water. "Penny" Jenkinson used to sell sea urchins at the start of the Brigg.

North of the Brigg, the headlands towards Scarborough have names such as Yons Nab, Horseshoe Rocks and Old Horse Rocks. Gristhorpe Bay is rocky, but Cayton has a sandy beach. There is a footpath on the cliff top from Church Ravine to Carr Naze. At the seaward end a steep way with steps leads down to the rocks. Inland is a Country Park with a caravan site and picnic areas; there is also a miniature golf course and a Nature Trail offers a rewarding walk. Guides can be obtained from the Caravan Office there, or from the Information Centre in John Street. The Cleveland Way starts here, and the 40 mile cliff top walk up the coast is very popular — (see the book, "The Cleveland Way", published by Dalesman).

"Plum pudding stones" are to be found. They are lumps of red clay with many pebbles imbedded. One very big one was called The Wishing Stone—you pulled out a pebble (with great difficulty) and made a secret wish.

FISHERMEN AND FISHING BOATS

A WRITER in 1815 described Filey as having between 500 and 600 inhabitants, the greater part of the population being composed of the fishermen and their families. Eight 5-man boats were usually sent from the town to the herring fishery at Yarmouth, a greater number than was employed by any other fishing town on the Yorkshire coast except Staithes. Scarborough could only manage three. In 1833 the yawls, of between 40 and 60 tons, went to the

Dogger Bank, 70 miles ENE of Flamborough. In 1897, Filey manned 34 yawls and 17 big herring cobles, which had a crew of four and weighed 25 tons. There were also 64 inshore cobles. Over 400 men earned their living from the sea, and scores of families helped.

In the early 1800s Filey was a rough place, and when preachers from Bridlington came with ideas of reformation they were pelted with dried fish. 1823 saw John Oxtoby in Filey and his zeal had some success. The first Wesleyan chapel was built in 1811 and the Primitive Methodists opened a church in 1824. The boats began to have names such as "Concord", and "Good Intent". There was no fishing on Sundays.

Wives and daughters gathered bait, walking four miles on the beach towards Cayton Bay for "flithers" (limpets). They carried them in a "maund", or basket. It was a cold wet task in winter. The wives rose at 5 o'clock to get the washing done before spending an arduous day bait gathering. In the evening they would skin the fish ready for baiting the lines the following day.

The fishermen held on to superstitions long after the Methodist conversion. A man baiting a line would stop if someone mentioned a pig. The crew of a boat would refuse to go to sea if the word "pig" was used in their presence. A black cat was considered unlucky, and a shopkeeper would close immediately if a customer asked for eggs for supper. It was once thought unlucky to rescue a drowning man. If a girl set the "First Foot" on New Year's Morning the chance of a good season's fishing was ruined.

There has been so much intermarriage that nicknames are given to many of the fishermen to avoid confusion among the Jenkinsons, Cammishes and Mainprizes. "Tich", "Laffy", "Scrat", "Ginger", "Crump", "Bonzo", "Mizer", and so on, are a few of them used over the years. There were wedding day customs. The bride and bridegroom would hold a silk handkerchief, and a crowd of men raced after it. Some of the runners had collections of these. A plate of wedding cake would be thrown over a bride's head to break on the ground. The more pieces there were, the more luck there would be. A funeral in Queen Street meant drawn blinds and a procession to the church with the mourners singing

A FILEY YAWL ON THE BEACH · 1840

SAILING COBLES

hymns all the way. A fisherman's coffin was carried by fishermen holding it by white slings. A woman was carried by women.

The fishing has fluctuated in prosperity, and the number of men employed has dwindled. In the late 1930s the number of cobles had dropped to below 40, and in 1953 there were only ten, with four keelboats operating from Scarborough with Filey crews. After the war, young men forsook the trade of their forebears for better paid and easier jobs, but there has been a revival in recent years and youngsters have come back to the boats. The cobles are bigger and better equipped. The men suffer less from the weather, and are protected by brightly coloured waterproofs and thigh boots. Around 50 men are now employed in fishing. There are fourteen 3-man cobles and three 2-man boats.

Launching and landing a boat at Filey is much more difficult than at places with a harbour. The cobles are pushed into the sea by the tractor, and one of the crew is usually in the water. On returning, one man has to drop over the side to attach the towing chains, and a big wave can drench him. The rudder is always removed inboard, after taking the tiller off, and the coble comes in stern first.

The salmon season lasts from May until October, and the nets, often draped over the railings or the wall of the landing, may be 320 yards long. Occasionally something bigger is caught, such as a basking shark weighing two tons and causing damage to the nets. Seals are a nuisance sometimes. Crabs and lobsters are caught in the summer. The "pots", made of wood by the fishermen, have a wooden floor about 24 inches long and 18 inches wide. The bows are young briars, with three to a crab pot and four for lobsters. A weight is fastened to the bottom and the pots taken out to sea in "fleets" of 25. A coble may carry around 200 pots piled high in the bows. Each fleet has two marker buoys, and the pots are anchored about 12 fathoms apart. The crew winch the pots to the coble to examine them. Sometimes rough seas can break the pots loose or damage them, and often the bait has not attracted a crab. Good catches bring good prices, but the return is uncertain.

THE COBLES

NOWHERE else in the world can such a craft as the Yorkshire coble be found. From the Viking longship, the Yorkshireman developed his open seaboat which could sail in rough weather, although it needed skilled hands. It has a high powerful bow and deep forefoot. Its wide clinker planking is painted in bright, contrasting colours. Designed to be launched from a wide, unprotected beach, it is a good surf boat, and once in open water it is a splendid seaboat.

Her ribs are of oak, with larch planks, and no steamed frames are used. She has no keel. The bigger boats seen at Scarborough and Bridlington are called "keelers", because they are different from the coble in this respect. She is built on a ram plank, carved from a solid balk and iron sheathed. Two skids protect the bottom aft, and between these the modern coble has its propellor. The narrow transom stern slopes steeply, and the long rudder, extending four or five feet below the bottom, gives a good grip of the sea.

The flat stern allows beaching to be carried out even in a heavy sea. The coble slides easily on the sand as big waves break over the bows. In sailing days there was a single dipping lug sail, hoisted by a well greased rope, on a mast raked at about 30 degrees. There was a shorter mast for use when the sail was reefed, and bags of shingle were carried as ballast. A typical coble in the 1890s was 27 ft. long and 7½ ft. wide, but no two were, or are, alike. They have for centuries been built to no plan except the owner's needs.

Filey has some sharp ended cobles, with the stern post steeply raked like the transom and retaining the long rudder. At one time these were called mules, and could also be seen at Scarborough. The Filey cobles were lighter in build than those at some places because of the need to handle them on to the low cranked axle wheels. The

BRINGING UP THE COBLES
In pre-tractor days, two or three horses were used. The wheels were wood.

Robin Hood's Bay crabbers were similar, as they had to be man-handled on wheels up the steep landing. There were once three boat builders in Filey. Small cobles, about 10 ft. long and called a "cauf" (calf), were carried on the bigger boats for long lining when fishing for cod.

I once heard a Filey fisherman say that he would sooner go out in his own coble than in the lifeboat. Yet the sea has claimed many a brave boat. In 1930 a south-east gale blew up during an August night, and several cobles were smashed or floated out to sea. More were damaged in the great gale of 1953, when spray drenched the look-out post on Carr Naze 180 ft. above the sea and the waves roared 60 ft. above the Brigg.

WRECKS

FILEY Bay is littered with wrecks from sailing days, and both world wars caused tragedies. There were 17 known sinkings between 1914 and 1918. At this time cobles fishing off Flamborough were sometimes accosted by German U-boats, whose crews, so it is said, bought fish from the Yorkshiremen. One coble, the *Edith Cavell,* was sunk by a U-boat and the crew were taken aboard. The captain questioned the coble men, and one boy, asked where he would have been if not at sea, replied: "At Sunday School, Sir." This pleased the captain, who later landed the crew safely in the Farne Islands. When they returned by train to Filey, half the town met them at the station.

In 1863 a great gale caused the loss of 24 fishing boats in the North Sea, and 144 men and boys died. In 1869, 90 vessels from Filey and Scarborough were caught by a gale and lost all their nets—34 Filey boats reached home safely, but three Scarborough boats were sunk. The loss to the two towns was £20,000, and 860 people were thrown out of work. In 1868 *The Beale,* a coal carrying brig, struck a rock one mile north of Filey. The crew took to a boat and were brought safely ashore by a coble. Many ships were wrecked in Filey Bay in 1696, and in 1740 nine ships were lost with two-thirds of their crew. In 1925 a steam drifter, the *Research,* sunk in Bridlington Bay and five of the lost crew were from one Filey family.

John Paul Jones, the famous American pirate, appeared off Flamborough to attack a British convoy of 41 ships. They were escorted by *HMS Serapis* and *The Countess of Scarborough.* The *Bonhomme Richard,* Jones' flagship, was sunk, taking with her the anchor from *Serapis*, and the convoy escaped. The people of Filey watched the battle from the cliffs by moonlight. Filey was attacked by a French ship in 1795. The local Volunteer Infantry, commanded by Squire Osbaldestone, drove off the French. In 1901 a trawler called *Dunrobin* fouled her nets in Filey Bay and the obstruction was found to be an anchor, thought to be the one from *Serapis*. It was put on display in Scarborough, but used for scrap during the last war.

A Norwegian steamer hit the Brigg in 1928, and although the crew were landed safely her cargo of herring was washed away. For some time after the Filey folk salvaged the boxes, and herring was the main meal in many houses.

THE LIFEBOAT

THE people of Filey decided to do something about saving lives in 1823, when they founded the lifeboat station, one year before the Royal National Lifeboat Institution was started. Since then 418 lives have been saved, and three awards won for bravery at sea. So have a look in the lifeboat house when it is open, and learn about the activities of this voluntary service which has been part of the lives of Filey folk for a long time.

The first boat, Scarborough built, cost £98 and was 30 ft. long with 12 oars. She served for 40 years and saved over 70 lives. The RNLI took over the service in 1852, and full records have been kept since then. Sometimes there have been two wrecks together. In 1857 a Whitby brig was driven ashore and the Filey lifeboat rescued her crew of nine. At the same time a schooner was driven on the beach, and

Robert Jenkinson, a fisherman, braved the high surf and threw a line on board, by which means the crew were rescued.

The Lord Mayor of York, R. W. Hollon, gave £250 towards a new lifeboat in 1862, and this was launched in the following year, bearing the donor's name. This was a self-righting boat, 33 ft. long with 10 oars. She was brought to Filey by train, with a procession of local dignitaries from the station. In 1874 the *Hollon* arrived too late to save the crew of a swamped coble, so the reward of £16 received from the RNLI was given to families of the men who died. When the *Hollon* was launched in March 1883 to aid a yawl in difficulties, a huge wave swung her broadside on as she slid from the launching carriage and she grounded. A large number of men waded into the breakers and succeeded in getting the boat's head to sea. They were all soaked by the icy waves. A new lifeboat, *Hollon the Second,* again paid for by the Lord Mayor and Mayoress of York, arrived on 13th September, 1884, and was taken in procession to the sands, where the vicar, Canon Cooper, conducted a service of dedication. A new lifeboat house was built in 1889, the one still in use today. *Hollon the Third* came in May 1907. She performed many rescues, including in 1912, taking off 33 passengers from the Scarborough pleasure steamer *Cambria* which had grounded on the Brigg in fog.

Three weeks after Lifeboat Day in August, 1930, when the sons of the Princess Royal went for a trip in the boat, one of the crew, John Willis, was run over and killed by the launching carriage. The launching continued, despite the tragedy, and the boat went to the assistance of a Yarmouth drifter aground in fog. May 1940 saw the arrival of a new lifeboat, *The Cuttle,* which was powered by a 35 hp petrol engine. It was launched 32 times during the war years. In 1943 there was a call out to help a tank loading-craft. As both cox and second cox were at sea, Richard Jenkinson, who had retired in 1935 after 20 years as cox, took the boat out. His crew spotted a mine only yards away from the landing craft. This danger was averted, and the lifeboat towed the casualty into Scarborough.

The *Isa & Penryn Milstead,* a new boat with twin diesel engines, arrived in 1953, and after many missions was replaced in 1968 with the *Robert and Dorothy Hardcastle.* which had a major refit in 1982. An inshore rescue boat arrived in 1966, and this was replaced in 1975. The ILB has been of great assistance to the big boat, and has carried out "rescues" of people in trouble on the Brigg. The fast moving craft can be launched very quickly in just two minutes.

An excellent book by Jeff Morris, called "Golf, Lima, Foxtrot, Echo" (the international call sign of the Filey lifeboat), can be obtained at the lifeboat house. It tells the full story of the gallant men and the boats they volunteer to serve in.

FILEY'S PARISH CHURCH

DESCRIBED as the finest church in the north-east corner of the old East Riding, St. Oswald's took fifty years to build. Its massive square tower, topped by a fish wind indicator, stands on the cliff top. Divided from the town by the deep Ravine, it is surrounded by a graveyard with old tombstones bearing interesting inscriptions.

The church dates from the reign of King Stephen, and was begun under the auspices of the Augustinian Canons from Bridlington Priory, founded by Walter de Gant and completed in 1114. St. Oswald carried the Gospel into Lincolnshire, and lived in Northumberland, so it is likely he passed through Filey, and from earliest times the church was dedicated to him. The original design was for a nave only, with a tower at the western end. The size of the western piers indicates this, as does the space left for a staircase in the western wall.

In the thirteenth century the original chancel and the eastern bay of the nave were taken down and an eastern extension built, with a chancel crossing and central tower and north and south transepts. The battlemented parapets were added in the 15th century. A unique feature is the chancel being built two steps lower than the nave. At one time the west end had a music gallery and organ. The ground below this was cobbled and sheep from a nearby

ST. OSWALD'S PARISH CHURCH

farm were allowed to eat the grass which grew between the stones. In 1908 a fire destroyed the organ and part of the roof, and the new organ was placed in the chancel. At one time, church music was provided by two violins and a cello.

In 1839, when the old oak seating and screen were removed, the walls were covered with several coats of white-wash, obliterating many ancient features. It is said that a carved figure on the south wall was preserved from demolition by the promise of a pint of ale to the workman. The ancient font was once kept locked. As the water was consecrated only once a year, it had to be protected from any profane use. On either side are places where pieces have been broken away.

The easternmost window in the south aisle is called the Fishermen's Window. Near it is a little carved figure, which is thought to be a memorial to a former "boy bishop" of Filey. He had to keep the boys of the parish in order from St. Nicholas' Day (December 6th) to Christmas Eve. Next to the modern altar is the ancient stone one, which has five crosses and a receptacle for relics. It was discovered in the floor of the aisle near the chancel door in 1925. At the time of the Reformation, these stone altars were taken from the sanctuaries and laid near a door "for all to walk over as they entered or left the church".

In 1885 a restoration was carried out by Mr. W. S. Barber, under the direction of Canon Cooper who was the vicar from 1880 to 1935. A specimen of the old stall headings was preserved and is to be seen in the south porch. The design for the new stalls was copied by Mr. Elwell, the celebrated carver, from Beverley Minster. the dedication taking place on August 5th, 1886, St. Oswald's Day. Canon Cooper was a well-known figure in Filey for many years. He became known as the "walking parson", and published several books describing his tramps in this country and abroad. In summer he gave lectures in the church for visitors about the history of the building and the town.

One of the church bells is cracked, from excessive use celebrating the war victories in Pitt's time. A tombstone bears the legend: "To Susannah Naggs She being dead yet speaketh". Memorials in the church bear many family names, and show the toll of life taken by the sea in the fishing community.

PLACES OF INTEREST AROUND FILEY

THE farmlands around the town rise to the Wolds behind Hunmanby, with the wooded hills to the north backed by the rolling moors of the North York Moors National Park. Many of the villages are unspoilt, and there are minor roads uncongested by traffic.

Muston: Less than two miles away, this village lies on the A1039 road which leads off the main A165 Scarborough road. A small place with some old cottages, it has a hall set in a fine garden with willow trees. The Ship Inn has curved gables. The church of All Saints dates from 1863, but has a Norman font. At one time Filey's letters were left here to be collected, and the church sent a minister to "supply" Filey church.

Hunmanby: Reached by a minor road from the A165, this is a big village with new housing on its fringes but a fine old main street. It was once a market town and is set on the wooded eastern slope of the Wolds. The name seems to be connected with hounds or dogs kept for hunting wolves. Chariot burials (two harnessed horses) were discovered here.

The hall was once the seat of the Osbaldestone family who were well known as hunting squires. Hunters were bred and there were regular race meetings. In the early 19th century, Humphrey Osbaldestone improved the grounds, started plantations and built new farmhouses. The hall is now a school for girls administered by the Wesleyan Educational Trust. The village has a reputation for longevity. In 1808, of the thirteen people who died in Hunmanby, five were over the age of 80. At the eastern end of the village is the ancient brick-built "lock up", and next to it the pinfold where stray cattle were impounded. The market was held on Tuesdays, but declined when the port of Bridlington began to prosper and Driffield grew with the cutting of the canal linking it to Hull.

The church of All Saints has a Norman tower, but there were restorations in 1845. There was a hospital attached to the church, "for one alderman, and fourteen brothers and sisters for the preservation of people travelling that way, that they might not be devoured by wolves, and other wild beasts, then abounding there." There is a cobbled floor to the porch, and monuments to the Osbaldestone family. Almost opposite the church is a wide area flanked by fine old buildings, including an inn, The Veterinary Arms (meals served).

There are riding stables in the village. Buses connect with Filey, Scarborough and Bridlington. The railway station is still open, with trains to Filey, Scarborough, Bridlington and Hull.

Flixton and Folkton: Both on the A1039, a couple of miles past Muston, these villages have picturesque cottages and attractive inns. From the Wolds to the south, there are wide views of Filey Bay.

Gristhorpe: Two miles from Filey on the inland side of the main Scarborough road. Old farmhouses and cottages have russet pantiled roofs, and the inn—The Bull—is an attractive old place. There is a caravan village nearer the cliffs, and Gristhorpe Bay has a rocky shore.

Cayton: About five miles from Filey, on a minor road off the A165, this is a larger village with new houses, and shops. The church has a Norman doorway. Cayton Bay a mile away, has a sandy beach enclosed by two headlands, Osgodby Point to the north and Yons Nab to the south. There is a car park near the main road by the Holiday Camp, and toilets.

There are three entries to Filey Bay other than at Filey itself. The first one, 1½ miles south, is **Primrose Valley**, where there is a big caravan site with cafes, amusements, heated swimming pool, shops, etc. A footpath leads down the tree clad ravine to the beach, and there is the "Primrose Puffer" a small train. Car park and toilet facilities available. Butlins Holiday Camp comes next, boasting Yorkshire's longest bar 198 ft. long with 20 beer pumps. The Camp is open to day visitors. **Hunmanby Gap**, further south, is reached by a lane from the A165. There is access to the sands, and a car park. **Reighton Gap** is just before the cliffs begin to rise. It has a car park, cafe and toilets.

Bridlington: A big and busy resort with splendid beaches, a fascinating harbour and all kinds of entertainments. There is an angling festival in September when the cobles are crowded with parties out for fishing. The old town has an interesting High Street, and a fine Priory Church, with the ancient, fortified Bayle Gate.

Sewerby Park: A mile towards Flamborough, from Bridlington, there are fine gardens, with miniature golf, bowls, etc., and a children's zoo. The hall is an art gallery. A little train runs to Sewerby from the end of the promenade, and there is also a cliff path.

Flamborough: The village stands inland from the great white cliffs of the headland. There are caves to explore, and the lighthouse. At the North Landing there is a small beach, and the cobles take visitors for views of the caves. At Danes Dyke, near Flamborough, there is a Nature Trail.

Bempton: Here the cliffs are high and vertical. This is a breeding ground for countless seabirds, and there is a gannet colony. Fulmars, kittiwakes, puffins, cormorants, guillemots and black-backed gulls can be seen and heard in great numbers. Access is from the village, but cars cannot be taken to edge of the cliffs. The Bridlington bus serves the village, and there is a railway station a quarter of a mile away.

Speeton: Just off the B1229, this is a tiny village, with one of the oldest churches in Yorkshire, half a mile away, in the middle of a field.

Scarborough: The town has everything for the visitor that a large resort can offer—good beaches, a picturesque harbour, a headland crowned by a ruined castle and cliff gardens. There are hotels, cafes, amusements, sea trips and plenty of ice cream, fish and chips, with county cricket thrown in during September.

MOTOR RUNS

Burton Agnes: A magnificent Elizabethan mansion set in extensive grounds, not far from Bridlington. Drive to Hunmanby, then on to Burton Fleming, and south to Rudston. In the churchyard here is the largest standing stone in Britain, 25½ ft. high. Winifred Holtby, whose book "South Riding" is a great favourite, came from Rudston. Her grave is in the churchyard—she died at the age·of 37. A secondary road leads to Burton Agnes, where the hall is open to the public in the afternoon. Return on the A166 towards Bridlington, turning left at Carnaby to Boynton Hall, built in the 16th century by the Stricklands. Sir William sheltered Queen Henrietta Maria after the bombardment of Bridlington by Parliamentary ships. One of the family brought the first turkeys to this country, and the lectern in the church is a monument to this. From Boynton drive north to Grindale and Reighton, turning left for Hunmanby and Filey.

Sledmere: From Filey drive on the A1039 to Muston and Staxton turning left here for Foxholes. Go straight across, and then at the next crossroads turn right, over the Wolds with wide views, into Sledmere. Built by the Sykes family in 1751, the mansion is open to the public. The Sykes were responsible for draining and timbering large areas of the Wolds. See the unusual Wagoners' Memorial in the village. Return by going north to Lutton and West Heslerton, and then on the A64 and A1039 back to Filey.

Troutsdale: This is a scenic drive, with places for a picnic. Drive to Seamer by way of Cayton village and then on to East Ayton. Turn left on the A170 to Ebberston. Look for a signpost, and turn sharp right. The road runs through splendid scenery, with steep hills and wide views, to Hackness. From this picturesque village, drive through Forge Valley back to East Ayton. An extension to this run can be made by turning left at Hackness to Silpho and by way of forest and moorland to the main Whitby road north of Cloughton. At the Falcon Inn turn off for Staintondale and Ravenscar, a small scattered village with a wonderful view of Robin Hood's Bay from the 600 ft. high cliffs. There is a Nature Trail here.

Flamingo Park: This zoo is a great place for youngsters. Drive on the A1039 and then the A64 to Malton. Turn north here on the A169 to Kirby Misperton, where you will see signposts for the zoo car park. Return by going north to Pickering, which has an interesting church and ruined castle, and then on the A170 to Thornton-le-Dale, a pretty village with a stream by the main street. Continue to East Ayton, where turn right for Filey.

Rievaulx Abbey: One of the finest Cistercian ruins in Britain. It lies near the old town of Helmsley, which has a wide market place and castle. The A170 from East Ayton takes you direct to Helmsley. On the way you can leave the main road to see beautiful Hutton-le-Hole, or Lastingham, which has a church with an ancient crypt.

Burnby Hall Gardens, Pocklington: These pleasant gardens and lakes are worth seeing and there is a museum. Drive to Seamer, and turn left on the A64 to Staxton. Here turn left on the B1249 and go across the Wolds to Driffield. From here follow the A163 through Kirkburn, and then go to the right on the B1246 through North Dalton and Warter (a pretty village) to Pocklington. The gardens are to the south of the town on the B1247. Return by driving north to Great Givendale to join the A166. Turn right, and at Fridaythorpe bear left on the B1251 for Sledmere. From here take the B1253 to Octon crossroads and then turn left on the B1249 back to Staxton. The gardens are open at weekends from Easter until the end of May and then daily (except Saturdays) until mid-September.

WALKS

ALTHOUGH the country around Filey is not quite the splendid walking ground to be found further north in the North York Moors National Park, it is pleasant enough and not difficult.

At low tide you can walk on the firm sands to Primrose Valley, once called "Mile Haven", or, if the sea covers them, on the cliff top. A steep, tree shaded path ascends to the edge of the caravan area, and joins the road, flanked by villas, which leads to the main road. A short walk on the footpath, turning right, crosses the railway, and very soon a lane turns right to Lowfield Farm. Follow this past the farm and through another caravan site. The path crosses the railway again and leads to the edge of the golfcourse. You can return to the town on West Avenue, or down Martins Ravine back to the beach.

A pleasant walk starts behind the lifeboat house, and goes up the cliff path and on Pampletine Cliffs through the Country Park. Turn right on Carr Naze, with splendid views of the cliffs and headlands towards Scarborough. Or turn left and go on the cliff edge past Gristhorpe, with the Castle Rocks and Old Horse Rocks visible at low tide. Then, at Yons Nab, Cayton Bay appears. The main road can be joined here, or if you are energetic you can follow the path now part of the Cleveland Way, to Scarborough. To shorten this walk there is a path from the cliffs, about a mile from Carr Naze, which leads back to the main road at the edge of the town.

The lanes around Muston and Hunmanby are quiet, apart from the high season, and the hedges are full of wild flowers with blackberries in September. A footpath from Hunmanby joins the main road near the level crossing. A short walk to the left brings you to the Lowfield Farm lane, mentioned in the first walk.

It is possible to walk all the way round the Bay to Flamborough, passing the huge cliffs at Bempton and Speeton. The distance is about 12 miles. The train can be used to return from Bempton station, or one can walk back to Speeton and catch the bus from Bridlington at the road junction a mile or so past the village.

Useful Map: Ordnance Survey Sheet 101 (1:50,000).